How to Do a Science Project and Report

How to Do a Science Project and Report

BY MARTIN J. GUTNIK

A GROLIER COMPANY

A Language Skills Concise Guide
FRANKLIN WATTS
New York | London | Toronto | Sydney | 1980

Library of Congress Cataloging in Publication Data

Gutnik, Martin J
How to do a science project and report.

(A Language skills concise guide)
Includes index.
SUMMARY: Discusses performing scientific re-
search following the eight steps of the scientific
method and writing a formal report of the results
following a special format.
1. Science—Experiments—Juvenile literature. 2.
Report writing—Juvenile literature. [1. Science—
Experiments. 2. Report writing. 3. Experiments]
I. Title. II. Title: Science project. III. Series:
Language skills concise guide.
Q164.G96   507'.2   80–14866
ISBN 0–531–04129–8

Diagrams by Vantage Art, Inc.

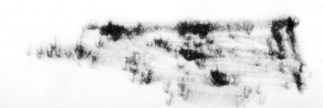

Contents

for
Liza, Andrew,
Max, and Anne

Introduction

Science is the accumulation of verified or proven facts or laws, put together in an orderly system in order to be communicated to other people.

Since all scientists are in the business of discovering and proving new laws or facts, and since their discoveries must be recorded either for themselves or for others, they must all follow an orderly procedure of scientific investigation. This procedure is called the *scientific method.*

A student preparing a science project must also follow certain steps or procedures in order to finish with valid results that others can and will accept. The student, too, must follow the scientific method.

Scientists perform science projects to extend the body of scientific knowledge. Students, too, may make new discoveries. Whatever the results, however, science projects are a superb way to satisfy a student's natural curiosity about the world.

IDENTIFYING A PROJECT

There are a myriad of science problems within the different disciplines of the science field. Each discipline—biology, chemistry, earth science, and so on—offers a great variety of existing science projects to choose from and perform. The one common denominator among all the science projects available is that they all must follow the scientific method.

In order for a science project to have meaning for oneself or others, it must be research-oriented. Within each scientific discipline there are an abundance of research problems to be performed. All one must do is ask a question, find the discipline, and then, according to accepted procedures, seek out an answer.

A research project utilizes all the tools of science on its path to a solution. Experiments have to be performed, records of observations must be kept, and an analysis of results must be made.

An example of a research problem is the question, "How do plants rid themselves of the water they absorb through their roots?" First, we identify the discipline. It is botany. In order to answer the basic question, many observations and experiments will have to be performed, and many other questions will have to be proposed and answered. We may or may not eventually arrive at a satisfactory conclusion. Not all science problems have answers. Either way, we will have satisfied some of our curiosity, acquired some valuable knowledge, and learned how to relate this knowledge to ourselves and to others.

THE PROCEDURES OF SCIENCE

As mentioned above, within the science field there are certain procedures involved in the acquisition of knowledge. These procedures are the very meat of scientific inquiry and discovery. They will guide you through your science project and help you to conduct your investigations. They are, briefly:

1. Observation
2. Classification of properties
3. Making an inference
4. Predicting
5. Formulating a hypothesis

6. Testing your hypothesis
7. Interpreting data (analyzing results)
8. Drawing conclusions and identifying variables

Science is a series of generalizations that cover a broad range of happenings. The above eight techniques of science should be used in all scientific investigations.

Chapter I.
Observation

To observe is to study an object or a situation with as many senses as possible. It is also to extend the senses, with the use of aids, as much as possible.

Observation is probably the most basic and necessary procedure within the investigation of scientific occurrences. In order to carry on a proper scientific inquiry, one must be able to observe events carefully.

There are many steps in the process of observation, but the first is research. Once you have identified a question or problem that you desire to investigate, you must attempt to discover what other people have already done with this problem. This aspect of your science project will be dealt with in the library, where you will gather relevant textbooks and journals. The information you obtain will be helpful to you with your own investigation and will decrease the chances of error.

SIGHT OBSERVATIONS:
THE UNAIDED EYE

As soon as your library research is completed, you will be ready for simple sight observations. This means simply observing visual phenomena within the realm of your problem and recording data. Here are some simple sight observations that were recorded:

MEALWORM METAMORPHOSIS		
DATE	OBSERVATION	ENVIRONMENTAL CONDITION
8/09/80	Mealworms, beetles present. No eggs.	Bed with carrots for moisture and burlap cover.
8/30/80	Beetles seem active. Many dead. More beetles than previously.	Added carrots to oatmeal for moisture.
9/10/80	Large numbers, live and dead, of beetles. Fewer mealworms. Many worms in pupae state. Presence of eggs discovered upon examination of oatmeal flakes with 40X stereo microscope.	Oatmeal and carrots added to bed.
9/21/80	Hardly any mealworms present. Large numbers of pupae and beetles. Dead beetles removed.	Bed in fine condition.
10/7/80	Complete absence of mealworms. Pupae have all transformed into beetles.	Oatmeal and carrots added to bed.
11/6/80	Larvae hatched. Thousands of tiny mealworms present. All beetles dead. Total metamorphosis approximately four months.	

The above log is one method of recording observations. There are many other methods available, such as a graph or a chart or just notes and, sometimes, illustrations. Through-out this book we will use examples of all the various kinds, to help you decide which method is best for you or for the project you have chosen.

SIGHT OBSERVATIONS
WITH A
COMPOUND MICROSCOPE

Following simple observations that can be made with the unaided eyes are observations that can be made through extensions of the sense of sight.

For example, a barometer will aid in the observation of air pressure, while a psychrometer will give relative humidity. A thermometer can measure air or water temperature, and a weather vane will record the direction of the prevailing winds.

The microscope, however, is one of the most useful tools of sight extension. A microscope allows us to view and study objects that would be impossible to see with our unaided eyes. These scientific tools, which help us to extend our sense of sight, are made up of lenses that magnify objects.

The word *microscope* comes from two Greek words, *mikros,* meaning small, and *skopein,* meaning to look at. The microscope was invented in the late sixteenth century.

All microscopes contain lenses. A lens is a clear substance that permits light rays to pass through it and at the same time bends these rays (refracts them) so as to distort the image being observed. Some lenses are glass; others may be plastic, oil, or water. But each refracts the light in order to magnify an image.

A compound microscope is a combination of two lenses, the *eyepiece* and the *objective,* that work together in order to produce a higher magnification. The magnification equals the multiplication of the eyepiece times the objective. For example, if your eyepiece is 10X and your objective 20X, you will observe objects at 200X their natural size.

Some compound microscopes possess their own light

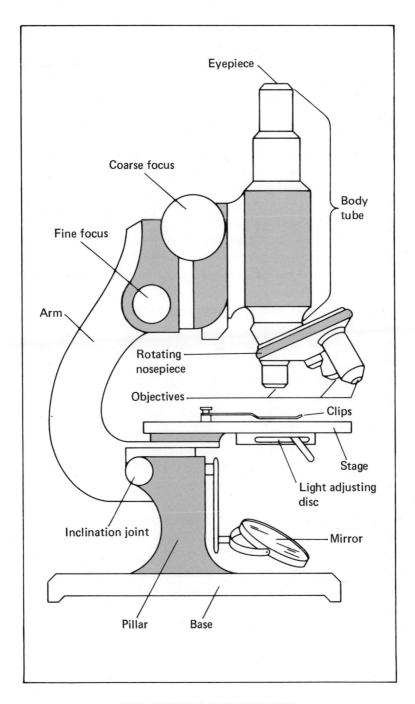

Eyepiece

Coarse focus

Body tube

Fine focus

Arm

Rotating nosepiece

Objectives

Clips

Stage

Light adjusting disc

Inclination joint

Mirror

Pillar   Base

THE COMPOUND MICROSCOPE

source (an illuminator) while others utilize room or natural light reflected off a mirror. The light, wherever it comes from, is passed through an aperture (opening) in the stage, through the object you are observing, through the objective lens, and finally through the body tube to the eyepiece. All objects studied under a microscope must be cut thin enough to permit light to pass through them.

If your compound microscope uses a mirror, place the microscope in an area with a great deal of light, preferably sunlight. Look through the eyepiece and, with both hands on the sides of the mirror, adjust the reflective glass until your eyepiece is flooded with white light.

Check your light-adjusting disc (sometimes called an iris) to ensure that it is set on number five, the maximum opening. This done, place your specimen (a leaf, a piece of tissue, or perhaps a root) on a glass slide on the stage over the opening and secure it with the metal clips. Look at it through the eyepiece to make certain you have placed it correctly. Now focus the specimen by placing your fingers on the coarse focus knobs (both left and right) and then, with your eye at the level of the stage, turn the knobs slowly away from you (lowering the tube) until the objective lens is about ⅛″ away from the specimen. Now, with your eye to the eyepiece, turn the knobs slowly toward you.

Note that the microscope should always be focused by moving the body tube *upward*. This avoids damaging slides or breaking a lens. Focus until you receive a relatively clear image.

This complete, grasp the fine focusing knobs (usually smaller than the coarse knobs) and turn them toward you and away from you until you receive the clearest possible image. Then rotate your light-adjusting disc in order to permit the proper amount of light to pass through your specimen. Some specimens require less light than others to be seen clearly.

You are now ready to study under the microscope the specimen you have chosen to observe.

A Plant Cell Observed
Under a Microscope

Every living organism is made up of cells. A cell is the smallest unit of living matter. Cells make up tissues. Tissues, in turn, make up organs and glands. All cells, both plant and animal, have certain aspects in common.

First, almost all cells contain a nucleus. The nucleus appears as a dark, shadowy portion within the perimeters of the cell wall. The nucleus is the control center for all cellular functions. This brainlike shadow is suspended in cytoplasm, a liquid found throughout the cell's interior.

All functioning parts of the cell (see pp. 10–11) move around in the cytoplasm. A vacuole is a sac within the cell, and chloroplasts (found in green plants) are floating bodies that contain chlorophyll.

The cell wall and cell membrane give the cell its shape and form as well as protect the delicate insides.

SIGHT OBSERVATIONS
FROM
EXPERIMENTATION

Scientific experiments, using proven laws, are also excellent instruments for studying events that cannot be detected through simple observation alone. For example, using the law that oxygen supports combustion, one can detect the presence of this colorless, odorless gas by plunging a glowing wood splint into an area where oxygen is suspected of being present. If the splint ignites, you have detected the presence of the gas. If not, one could assume that the gas is not present in its pure state.

Chemicals also serve as useful extensions of the sense of sight. Cobalt chloride test paper, for example, is used to test plants for transpiration of water, while Benedict's solution turns an orangy-brown in the presence of glucose (sugar).

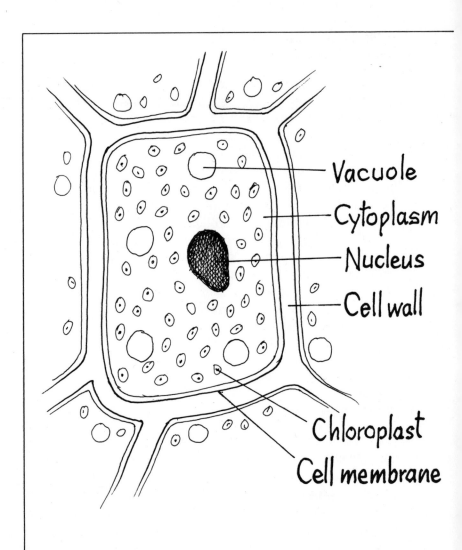

Vacuole
Cytoplasm
Nucleus
Cell wall

Chloroplast
Cell membrane

A PLANT CELL

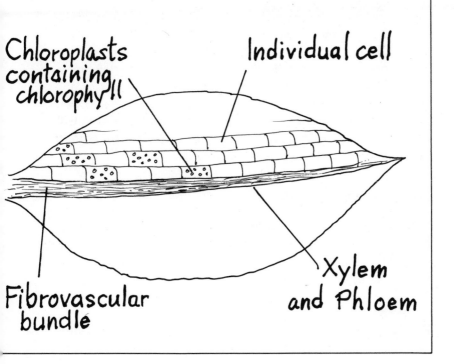

Chloroplasts
containing
chlorophyll

Individual cell

Fibrovascular
bundle

Xylem
and Phloem

Transpiration

Green plants, the only living objects on earth that can produce their own food, do so through the process of photosynthesis. In this process a green plant receives water through its roots, carbon dioxide gas through its stomata, and energy in the form of light. The chlorophyll found within the plant cell's chloroplasts converts the light energy to chemical energy. This chemical energy, which is stored in "energy-rich" molecules known as ATP, splits the water molecules that are within the plant. Some of the oxygen, liberated by the splitting of the water molecule, is released through the plant's stomata as breathable oxygen (O_2). Oxygen from the carbon dioxide that enters the leaf through the stomata combines with hydrogen, again from the splitting of the water molecule, and forms water. This water is released through the plant's stomata. The whole process is identified as *transpiration*.

In order to prove that plants transpire water, take a 2-inch (5-cm) square of cobalt chloride test paper and place it in a 3-inch (7.5-cm) square piece of cellophane. Hold the papers in place with a tweezers (to prevent moisture from your fingers reacting with the chemicals) and fold them in half (see p. 14). Now place the test paper on the leaf of any green plant—secure it to the leaf with a paper clip—and wait one day for results. The blue cobalt chloride test paper will change to pink, indicating the presence of moisture—a good sight observation for a science project.

TOUCH OBSERVATION

Observation through touch is another method for observing scientific or natural phenomena. Besides seeing the object, one can determine its texture and density as well as its molecular (physical) state.

Turgidity

Plants, all living things for that matter, depend upon water for their existence. Water serves as an internal transportation

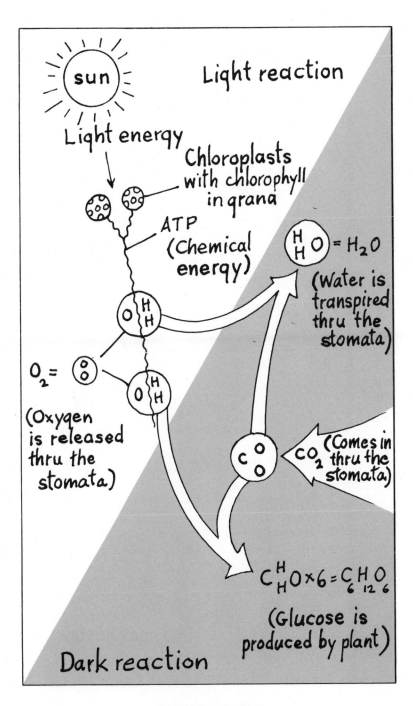

PHOTOSYNTHESIS

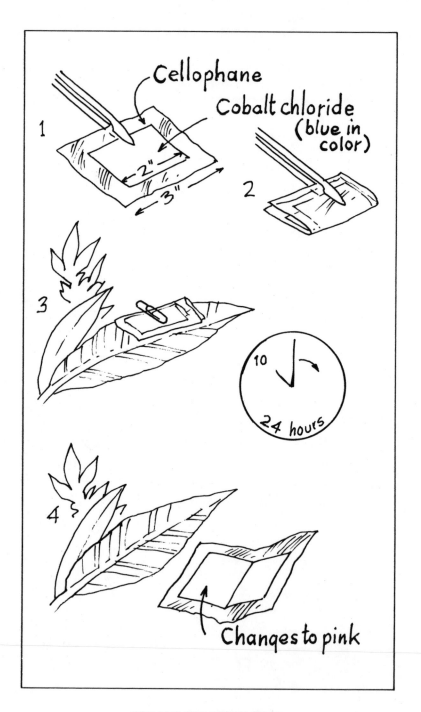

COBALT CHLORIDE TEST

system for almost all organisms. In animals, water is necessary to form the liquid of the circulatory system, the system that transports the essential nutrients of life throughout the organism's body. In plants, water is required for the process of photosynthesis, the production of food and oxygen for all living things.

In plants, because they do not have a skeleton, water is necessary to support the cells, to give them shape and form. When a plant is filled with water and firm, it is said to be *turgid.*

Plant two coleus (or almost any other green plant) in two separate pots. Examine the leaves and stems of each plant with your fingers. Bend them over gently and then let go. Do they spring back? If so, then the plant is turgid.

Water one of the coleus plants thoroughly and place it in a well-lit location. Do not water the other plant and place it next to the first. Wait a week. Water the first pot as often as necessary, but do not water the second pot.

At the end of the week, examine each plant with your fingers. Does one, the one without water, feel limp and lifeless? Does it spring back? If not, then it is not turgid.

Scientists use all their senses for keen observation of natural or scientific phenomena. Naturalists observe nature, physicists observe the atom, and chemists observe elements and compounds. Whatever discipline you choose to work within for your science project, observation is the first and key step along the scientific path to discovery.

Chapter II.
Classification
of Properties

To classify is to place objects into meaningful groups based upon their properties. A property is anything that belongs to an object and identifies that object as a unique entity.

All phenomena observed during a science project must be classified. For example, gases, liquids, and solids are the three physical states of matter. All objects can and should be classified into one of these three groupings, depending upon the state of the object's molecular configuration.

CLASSIFICATION OF THE
PHYSICAL STATES OF MATTER

A *solid* is any object that has its own shape and form and whose molecules, which are dense in configuration, move very slowly.

A *liquid* is any object that takes the shape of its container and whose molecules, which are of a medium density, move at a medium speed.

A *gas* has no shape or form and fills any available space. Its molecular density is low, and the speed at which the molecules move is rapid.

ECOLOGICAL CLASSIFICATIONS
OF SYMBIOTIC RELATIONSHIPS

Symbiosis is a close (dependent) relationship between two or more living things. This dependence, in most cases, is so necessary that the organisms involved usually cannot exist without each other. Symbiosis is an important ecological relationship. Without it many types of organisms would cease to exist.

Mutualism

Mutualism is a form of symbiosis in which all the organisms involved benefit.

ORGANISMS	RELATIONSHIP
1. The bee and the flower	A bee uses the flower's pollen in order to manufacture honey. In turn, while the insect is traveling from bud to bud, it carries on its legs pollen which, because of rubbing or collision, drops off, and thus fertilizes other flowers. Many species of plants could not reproduce if it were not for bees and other insects.
2. The tic bird and the rhinoceros	The tic bird sits upon the rhinoceros's back and, with the large herbivore's permission, of course, eats all the pesky little insects that have buried their heads within the mammal's body and have begun to suck its blood. The bird benefits with a meal and the rhinoceros benefits by the removal of the pests.

Commensalism

A form of symbiosis in which one organism benefits and the other is neither helped nor harmed is called *commensalism.*

ORGANISMS	RELATIONSHIP
1. Salamander and garter snake	A garter snake will utilize an abandoned salamander den for hibernation or protection. The salamander, who already has another home, is not helped or harmed. The garter snake benefits.
2. Moss and a tree	Moss, in order to obtain sunlight and moisture, attaches itself to the trunk of a tree. The moss benefits while the tree is neither helped nor harmed.

Parasitism

Parasitism is a form of symbiosis in which one organism benefits at the expense (injury or death) of another. Parasitism should not be confused with predation. In predation, a predator kills and eats its prey immediately or soon afterward. A parasite lives off its host (the animal or plant harmed) while the host is still alive.

ORGANISMS	RELATIONSHIP
1. Lamprey eel and trout	The eel attaches itself through a sucker-like mouth to its host, the trout, and obtains sustenance from the trout's blood until the trout finally dies.
2. Streptococcal bacteria and people	The bacteria establish a colony in a human throat and thrive within its dark, warm, moist confines. The host suffers until the parasite is ultimately destroyed. If the parasite is not destroyed it will eventually destroy the host.

All scientific observations in a science project must be classified according to whatever groupings are appropriate within the discipline. A chemist would be interested in solids, liquids, and gases; an ecologist might be concerned with living and nonliving, biosphere classifications, and ecosystems. But no matter what the field, a science project, in order to be meaningful, must have all of its information properly classified.

Chapter III.
Making an Inference and Prediction

The third step involved in a science project is the inference. A reasonable assumption based on past experience, the inference is an extension of your observation and a result of the process of creative and critical thinking. In order to carry on any scientific inquiry, one must be able to make logical inferences. An inference can be defined as an educated guess based upon facts or evidence of a past event or phenomenon.

The process of inference is not utilized by scientists alone. Historians, psychologists, and many other professionals, including, of course, criminal investigators, all use inferences in their daily work. A broken window, a red splotch on the floor, drawers askew, the front door ajar—what would a detective infer from observing these circumstances?

Scientists make inferences about the behavior of natural or scientific phenomena based upon what they observe. For example, naturalists have inferred from their study of ecosystems that all organisms fit into a definite food web that, if disturbed, will upset the entire balance of the natural order.

THE KAIBAB DEER STORY:
AN INFERENCE GONE BERSERK

There is a forest in Arizona, its name Kaibab, where deer flourished along with wolves, coyotes, cougars, and many other small animals, insects, and birds. This forest was a place of serenity and beauty. It was frequented by people from all over the United States—campers, anglers, travelers, and hunters. All enjoyed the forest's offerings; most felt a strong kinship with nature when they were in the forest.

But the hunters complained there were not enough deer. The wolves and cougars, especially the cougars, killed far too many, and there was little left for sport. These hunters, through their publications and political representatives, managed to make their voice heard in the Arizona state legislature. It was *inferred* that if the cougars were removed the deer would flourish, and the forest would become a haven for hunters.

The lawmakers complied, and a bounty was put on the heads of all the cougars within the state of Arizona. This done, the destruction commenced. The large cats were relentlessly hunted and murdered until, not long after the legislation went into effect, they were extinct within the borders of the state.

At the time the cougar legislation was passed, there were approximately 4,000 white-tailed deer in the Kaibab Forest. Two years after the destruction of the cougars the number of deer had increased to 7,000 and two years after that to 11,000. The hunters were overjoyed.

But the following winter, tragedy struck. As the snow fell and temperatures plunged, the forest's food supply dwindled. The deer, as they did every winter, ate branches, bark, and whatever plants were available. But there was not enough. There were too many deer. The number of deer had surpassed the forest's carrying capacity. That winter 4,000 of the 11,000 deer in the herd died of starvation. The winter after that, another 2,000 died, and another 2,000 after that. The herd was eventually reduced to 3,000 deer.

It was a bitter lesson for the hunters and naturalists. They discovered that predation is necessary for the balance of nature. They also discovered that inferences about nature should not be used to prescribe action until thorough studies are conducted to test the action for its environmental impact.

INFERENCES WITHIN
OTHER DISCIPLINES

Other inferences within different fields include statements on the behavior of gases or liquids; the effects of radiation on the body; and the possibilities of developing solar energy.

No matter what the discipline, the inference is a key step in any scientific investigation. It becomes the goal stated and guides the rest of the investigative process. Your inference will set your science project on its way toward a resolution.

PREDICTION

Prediction is an educated guess, based upon observation, about an event or phenomenon that is going to happen. A meteorologist, based upon his or her knowledge of air and past and present observations of atmospheric patterns, predicts weather conditions.

Your prediction or inference becomes the key to the next step within the scientific process, the formulation of a, hypothesis.

Chapter IV.
Your Hypothesis

The hypothesis is an extension of the inference or prediction. It is the initial step in the performance of an actual scientific investigation. Like the inference or prediction, the hypothesis is based upon observation, and, like the inference or prediction, it is a statement about something that has happened or that will happen. The major difference is that a hypothesis must be able to be tested. It is a provable or nonprovable statement (usually an *if-then* statement) about events or phenomena that have occurred or that will occur.

A HYPOTHESIS CONCERNING
TEMPERATURE INVERSION

Observation and Research

Smog, a combination of pollutants, smoke, and water vapor in the atmosphere, is exceptionally dangerous to human health during the phenomenon of a temperature inversion.

Our atmosphere usually rids itself of pollutants through movement. Air moves in two ways, by wind and by convection. Convection is the term used to describe the movement of air when heated. It is a basic fact that cool air, being heavy, falls, and warm air, being light, rises. This pattern of movement—the rising and falling—is called a convection current and serves to circulate atmospheric gases upwards and downwards. As the warm air rises it becomes cooler and heavier until it falls.

Under normal conditions the air close to the earth's surface is warmer than the air at higher altitudes. This air, through the process of convection, rises and is replaced by the cleaner, fresher, cooler air higher up.

A temperature inversion occurs when a warm air mass, its temperature higher than the surface air, settles above the surface air. This mass prevents the normal process of convection. The surface air is trapped, along with all the wastes of civilization it is shrouding. On days when there is no wind, a temperature inversion can be devastating. With the pollutants of the cities not being carried away, the air that we breathe becomes lethal.

Classification
A temperature inversion is the phenomenon of a warm air mass, its temperature higher than the surface air mass, settling above the surface mass and thus preventing the process of convection.

Prediction
Since air moves by convection, especially on days when there is no wind, a temperature inversion will prevent this phenomenon and entrap in the atmosphere any environmental pollutants.

Hypothesis
If a warm air mass, with temperatures higher than the surface air, settles above the surface air, then a temperature inversion will occur, entrapping all surface pollutants within the inversion.

Experiment Plan
a. *Materials Needed:* (1) a large bell jar (or mayonnaise jar); (2) ice cubes; (3) a light bulb and socket; (4) a tightly rolled piece of paper; (5) matches; (6) water.

TEMPERATURE INVERSION

b. *Methods:* Fill the bell jar approximately one-sixth full with cool water and then add enough ice cubes to cover the entire bottom of the jar. Allow the ice cubes, those in the jar, to sit for about two minutes. This will sufficiently cool the air mass (surface air) at the bottom of the jar.

This done, plug in the light bulb and socket and hold the illuminated bulb approximately 6″ (15 cm) above the mouth of the jar. The bulb must remain stationary until the experiment is completed.

Now take the tightly rolled paper and ignite it. Allow it to burn for about thirty seconds and then blow it out. The paper should now be smoking profusely. Drop the smoking paper into the jar.

Observe what happens to the smoke. Record and diagram your observations. Draw conclusions based on your hypothesis and experimental findings.

A HYPOTHESIS CONCERNING THE PROCESS OF PHOTOSYNTHESIS

Observations and Research
Only green plants carry on the process of photosynthesis. Green plants contain chlorophyll. Chlorophyll is the only substance on earth that is capable of converting light energy into chemical energy. All green plants require water, carbon dioxide, and light energy for the process of photosynthesis.

Prediction
Since all green plants are living, and in order to sustain themselves must carry on the process of photosynthesis, they will die if denied the basic nonliving ingredients for this process.

Hypothesis
If green plants are denied raw materials, water, carbon dioxide, and light energy (one or all), then they will not be able to carry on the process of photosynthesis.

a. Materials Needed

Jar

Ice cubes

Light bulb and socket

Rolled up paper

Water

Matches

b. Methods:

2 min

(turn page)

TESTING TEMPERATURE INVERSION

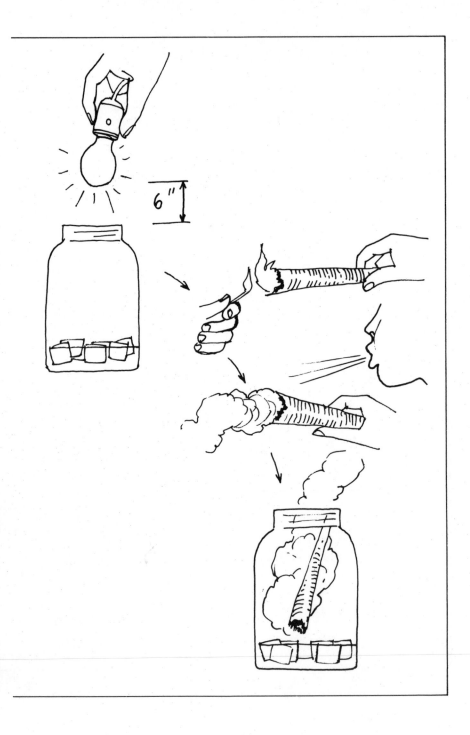

This hypothesis is, as stated previously, the first step for your scientific experiment. Once your hypothesis is formulated you must think of the best way in which testing can be completed.

Research will help you to decide on the type of experiment you want to perform and on what kind of experiment is the most feasible as far as equipment and time are concerned.

Every scientific investigation requires specific materials in order for the project to be completed. Sources to obtain needed materials can usually be identified by science teachers, science texts, or library research. But there may be times when equipment will have to be designed or devised by you yourself. Here is an example of a simple experiment plan:

1. *Hypothesis:* If a green plant produces sugar (glucose), then when boiled in Benedict's solution it will turn an orangy-brown in color.

2. *Materials:* Any green plant (stem and leaves), a large (500 ml) beaker, alcohol, alcohol burner, Benedict's qualitative solution, a measure, paper towels, a burner pad, and safety goggles.

3. *Methods:* I will take a section of green plant, the stem and leaf, and place it in a beaker of boiling alcohol in order to remove the chlorophyll. This done, I will remove the plant and dry it carefully on a paper towel. Then I will immerse the plant in a beaker of Benedict's solution and bring it to a boil. This done, I will analyze my results.

Chapter V.
Testing Your
Hypothesis

Once the hypothesis and materials have been established for your experiment, the next and most crucial step is the testing of your theory, the experiment itself.

This portion of your science project becomes the log or record of what you did to prove or disprove your hypothesis.

Hypothesis

If a moist piece of steel wool is exposed to pure oxygen over a period of 72 hours, then the oxygen and iron will combine to form the compound ferric oxide (rust).

Materials

A large pan, water, yeast, hydrogen peroxide, flask, stopper, delivery tube, steel wool.

Testing (What I did)

I filled a pan two-thirds full with water and then filled a test tube brimming with water. Carefully I placed my thumb over the mouth of the test tube, and then I placed the tube upside down in the pan of water. Once the test tube was beneath the surface of the water in the pan, I removed my thumb. The water, because of equalized pressure, remained in the test tube.

It is important that when logging or recording how you performed your experiment you be accurate and detailed. This will help others to comprehend your work and, if they so choose, to follow your methods.

> *I spread a thin layer of yeast on the bottom of a flask and then added fifty ml of hydrogen peroxide. Then I quickly capped the flask with a cork and delivery tube, placing the delivery tube under the test tube in the pan of water. This will allow the oxygen gas produced. . . .*

When explaining a very complicated procedure it is usually helpful to include a diagram. Sometimes an illustration, properly labeled, is all you really need to explain your process.

Chapter VI.
Interpreting Data

From the inception of your science project you have been gathering data. This data should be recorded and later gleaned for significance. All results of experiments—qualitative or quantitative—should be logged and considered an integral aspect of the science project.

DATA GATHERED FOR EVIDENCE OF THE FOOD CHAIN IN OUR ENVIRONMENTAL SYSTEM			
	WATER (pond)	BOG	UPLAND
PRODUCERS	All green plants, specifically fern, brush, and deciduous trees. Also all water plants.		
HERBIVORES	Tadpole	Fruit fly, red worm	Finch, fruit fly
CARNIVORES	Bluegill, black bass	Garter snake, leopard frog	Garter snake, leopard frog
OMNIVORES	Crayfish, turtle	Turtle, certain worms	Certain worms
DETRITUS (all dead or decaying material)	Fungi, bacteria, certain worms and flies		

RESULTS OF PHOTOSYNTHESIS EXPERIMENT WITH COLEUS PLANTS			
	CHLOROPHYLL	TURGIDITY	GLUCOSE
CONTROL GROUP	Large, healthy chloroplasts, dark green due to dense dispersal	Very turgid	A rich amount
NO CO_2	A noticeable sparseness, with a large amount of yellowing	Flimsy	Very little
NO H_2O	Chloroplasts broken apart, pale green color	Total lack of turgidity	None
NO LIGHT	Very pale, chloroplasts disintegrating	Still relatively turgid	None

RESULTS OF EXPERIMENT IN AN INDUSTRIALIZED AREA'S TEMPERATURE INVERSION

Because of the density of the cold air mass and the ceiling of warm air above it, convection (the movement of air up and down) ceases, and any pollutants in the cooler ground air become trapped. This phenomenon is called photochemical smog and is produced when hydrocarbons and the oxides of nitrogen combine in the air in reaction to the sun's ultraviolet light.

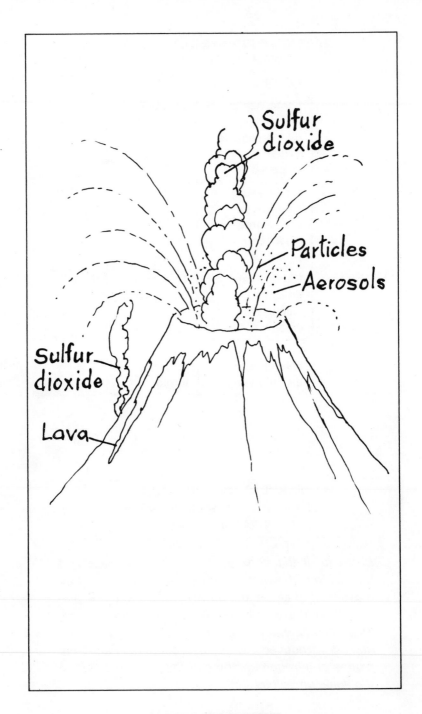

VOLCANO EXPERIMENT

```
┌─────────────────────────────────────────┐
│          RESULTS OF EXPERIMENT            │
│        IN NATURAL AIR POLLUTION:          │
│              A VOLCANO                     │
└─────────────────────────────────────────┘
```

Particles: 300 per square inch.
Aerosols: 2,000 per square inch.

Sulfur dioxide gas also present because lead acetate paper when moistened and exposed to smoke turned grayish-black.

Chapter VII.
Drawing Conclusions
and
Identifying Variables

As you approach the culmination of your work, your observations, demonstrations, research, and experiments start to come together as an organized conglomeration of data.

Was your hypothesis correct? Why? Why not?

You may not be able to answer the above questions. Many science projects finish by demonstrating a need for further investigation.

Also, did you take into consideration all the variables affecting your results and thus your conclusions?

Every conclusion must include how the variables affected or might have affected the scientific validity of the experiment. Variables are essentially those outside factors that may alter or distort your results. If the variables are not measurable or are too numerous to list, then your project conclusions must state this.

VARIABLES AFFECTING TEMPERATURE INVERSION
1. Wind speed (in the classroom or laboratory)
2. Air temperature
   a. At surface of jar
   b. At mouth of jar
3. Pollutants in air
4. Intensity of light bulb
5. How tightly the paper is rolled
6. Individual experimenter's error

CONCLUSION

My hypothesis was correct. A temperature inversion will prevent normal convection and thus will result in the surface air being inundated with dangerous, sometimes lethal, pollutants.

It was difficult to measure the amount of effluent within the temperature inversion due to the lack of sophisticated equipment. Nevertheless, it was observed that this phenomenon can be devastating to the inhabitants of any industrial society.

VARIABLES AFFECTING VOLCANO EXPERIMENT

1. Wind speed and/or convection currents.
2. Particles already in air.
3. Aerosols already in air.
4. Amount of sulfur in match heads.
5. Size of opening in individual clay volcanoes.
6. Individual experimenter's error.

CONCLUSION

My hypothesis was correct. Volcanoes do emit sulfur dioxide gas and particle and aerosol waste into the atmosphere, but due to ineffective measuring devices it was impossible to determine how much of this waste was from the volcano and how much was there beforehand.

It is this experimenter's suggestion that the experiment be repeated with more control over the atmospheric variables.

Always admit to possible error or a lack of variable control. This does not lessen the validity of your project, but rather it increases the possibility of its significance to yourself and others. Most scientific investigations have results that deviate somewhat from the original goal. That's how penicillin was discovered! Note the deviations and continue on toward your conclusion.

Chapter VIII.
The Formal Report

Any science project must follow the eight steps of scientific discovery, and all science projects should be written up in a formal report. That report must follow a special format and must include:

1. Observations
2. Research and all sources consulted; materials and methods used
3. Classification of all data
4. Any inferences or predictions made
5. Your hypothesis
6. Any results of experiments
7. Any conclusions reached
8. Any variables encountered
9. A display of your project

All reports must start with a formal statement of the problem and then a discussion of your observations. Your log of observations should be included within this section, as it relates to dates and times of significant discoveries or experiments. Here is an example of a log included in a formal report:

Problem: Analysis of the environmental and time requirements for leopard frog gestation (term of pregnancy) and development of the larval stage.

DAILY RECORD		
DATE	OBSERVATION	STATUS OF ECOSYSTEM
4/19/80	Eggs laid in jellylike base on elodea plant	Laid at edge of pond in still, protected water. Water cool and clear. Water temperature 56.4° F
4/24/80	Small, dark spots now appear in jellylike material	Weed condition sparse. Water temperature up 1.5° F
4/29/80	Dark spots seem to have grown, covering more of each individual egg. Jellylike material still intact	Some duckweed now growing on surface near the pond's edge. Water temperature up .79 of a degree
5/04/80	Upon close examination differentiation between a head and tail can be made inside the eggs. No movement. Jellylike material still intact	Infusion of duckweed well underway. Water temperature up 2.4° F. Some algae beginning to tint water green
5/07/80	Jellylike material beginning to disintegrate. Movement of tadpoles inside eggs	Duckweed and algae seem stable. Water color greenish-brown. Water temperature up 3.2° to 64.29° F
5/11/80	Breakup of jellylike material as tadpoles come out of eggs and float to bottom of pond	Water temperature up 2.6° to 66.89° F

Once you have tested your hypothesis and set it down formally in your report, you should then list any sources of information consulted:

Gutnik, Martin J. *The Life Cycle of a Leopard Frog.*
School resource. Science Library. Unpublished.

Your final written report should include an orderly listing of the classifications of your data. This will help anyone who is going to examine your work to understand the complexities and solutions of your problem.

pH RATINGS FOR
COMMON HOUSEHOLD PRODUCTS

	pH NUMBER	ACID	BASE
1. Vinegar	4	X	
2. Ammonia	12		X
3. Orange juice	5	X	
4. Aspirin	5	X	
5. Alka-Seltzer	6	X	
6. Bromo Seltzer	5	X	
7. Tide	6	X	
8. Borax	6	X	
9. Water	7	neutral	
10. Coffee	6	X	

Now, with the problem presented, observations recorded, research completed and listed, and classifications graphed, it is time to present your inference or prediction. Based upon your observations and classifications, your inference or prediction brings together all the information you have computed and reorganizes it into a meaningful statement of how you intend to deploy your intellectual efforts to find a solution.

Your hypothesis should be presented in the form of an *if-then* statement. An extension of your inference or prediction, the hypothesis must be able to be tested.

Hypothesis

If green plants produce glucose through the process of photosynthesis, then they must have, within their separate cells, structures (chloroplasts) that contain chlorophyll, an energy intensive substance that converts light energy into chemical energy.

Materials

Elodea leaf, geranium leaf, compound microscope, two blank slides, alcohol, ringstand, burner pad, 500 ml beaker, prism, flashlight, paper towels, test tube, cork, cardboard, and pin.

Methods

Through my observation, research, and classifications I discovered that green plants (producers) are the only organisms within the biosphere that possess the capability of producing food (glucose). They produce food not only for themselves but also for all other organisms within the biosphere. (See observations, research, and classifications previously stated.)

Green plants have the ability to produce glucose due to a substance within their tissues called chlorophyll. This substance (chlorophyll) is the only thing on earth that can capture light energy and convert it into chemical energy, thus enabling the plant to carry on the process of photosynthesis (food-making).

Having this data at my disposal, I inferred that since all green plants have this substance chlorophyll, it must be found within the separate cells of their tissues. Also, in order for it to be energy intensive, chlorophyll must have the ability to absorb the energy of light.

(Exp. 1.) Thus, procuring an elodea leaf from a culture in the school aquarium, I placed it in a drop of

water on a blank slide with a cover slip on top. I then put the slide on the stage of a compound microscope and observed the leaf under the 200X magnification (see results #1).

(Exp. 2.) I then took a geranium leaf and placed it in a beaker of boiling alcohol (chlorophyll is not soluble in water but will dissolve in alcohol). I allowed the leaf to remain until all its chlorophyll was extracted and suspended in the alcohol. I removed the now pale-yellow leaf and examined it, using the same procedure as above for chloroplasts (structures) containing chlorophyll (see results #2).

(Exp. 3.) Now I poured some of the chlorophyll extract from the above procedure into a test tube and corked the top, then took a piece of tagboard and with a pin made a small hole in its center. I taped this piece of tagboard over the top of a flashlight so that only a very small beam would emanate when it was turned on.

With the test tube of chlorophyll extract, a flashlight prepared as stated above, and a prism, I went into another room. There I turned off all room lights and turned on the flashlight. I held the prism, apex down, in the beam of white light being emitted from the flashlight. A spectrum was formed on the ceiling. Now I held the test tube of chlorophyll extract between the flashlight (in the beam) and the prism (see results #3).

Results

Your results emanate directly from the experiment and relate back to your methods. It is important that the results of your observations and experiments be recorded accurately.

(Exp. 1.) I observed chloroplasts within the separate cells of the plant. In the chloroplasts I ob-

Experiment 1

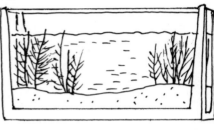

Experiment 2

Alcohol

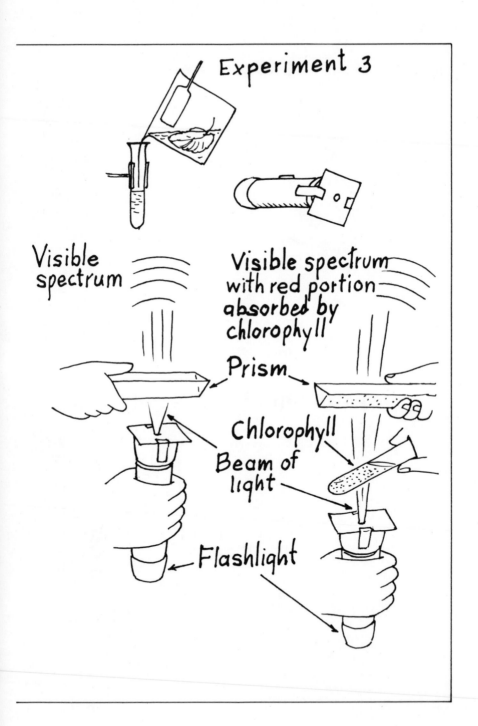

served grana (disclike) compartments containing the green pigment chlorophyll.

(Exp. 2.) *There was a complete absence of chlorophyll.*

(Exp. 3.) *The chlorophyll extract absorbed the radiant (red) portion of the visible spectrum.*

Conclusions

The summation of your work relates back to the original problem and, more directly, to the hypothesis. Conclusions are not necessarily supportive of your hypothesis nor do they always present a solution to the problem. Often conclusions lead you toward further exploration or other questions.

Successful scientific investigation does not necessarily coincide with the successful solution to an original problem but rather with new discoveries and an awareness of the variables involved in a particular phenomenological field.

While pondering your conclusions, you should record all observations and experiment variables (errors) that could have affected your results. It is virtually impossible to conduct a scientific investigation without variable error. Some of these variable errors are errors in measurement, errors in assessing environmental conditions, errors due to personal perspectives or biases, acidity, and individual organism characteristics.

No two things within the biosphere are exactly the same. Individuality extends from human beings to mice to plants to rocks and even to water molecules.

In order to be a conscientious scientific investigator, one must always allow for error due to object individuality and make others aware of this variable while writing conclusions.

If you will be displaying your project to your teacher, your class, or in public, you should make sure that your report is typed, mimeographed, and copies given to observers so that they can easily follow your oral or visual explanation.

Set up your display as attractively as you can, using all the available space without making the area appear cluttered. Use colorful tagboard or construction paper and title and label all the important aspects of your project.

Remember that while you are familiar with your project, others are not. Therefore it is very important that you communicate all the necessary information to those observing it in a thorough yet uncomplicated manner. Communication of your observations and discoveries is an important part of your science project, as important as was the investigation itself.

Appendix A.
A Bibliography for Project Ideas

Grossman, Shelley, Mary, and Louise. *Ecology* (The How and Why Wonder Books). New York: Wonder Books, 1971.

Gutnik, Martin J. *Ecology and Pollution—Air.* Chicago: Children's Press, 1973.

————. *Energy: Its Past, Its Present, Its Future.* Chicago: Children's Press, 1975.

————. *How Plants Make Food.* Chicago: Children's Press, 1976.

————. *What Plants Produce. Chicago:* Children's Press, 1976.

Hillcourt, William. *Activities and Conservation* (Field Book of Nature). New York: G. P. Putnam's Sons, 1961.

How and Why Wonder Book of Chemistry, The. Columbus, Ohio: Charles E. Merrill Books, 1961.

Hungerford, Harold R. *Ecology: The Circle of Life.* Chicago: Children's Press, 1971.

Moore, William. *Your Science Fair Project.* New York: G. P. Putnam's Sons, 1964.

Simon, Seymour. *Science Projects in Ecology.* New York: Holiday House, 1972.

————. *Science Projects in Pollution.* New York: Holiday House, 1972.

Smith, Norman F. *The Atmosphere.* Austin, Texas: Steck-Vaughn Company, 1975.

Wyler, Rose. *First Book of Science Experiments.* New York: Franklin Watts, 1971.

Appendix B.
Famous Science Projects
of the Past

As has been stated previously, science is the accumulation of proven facts or laws, put together in an orderly system in order to be communicated to other people. Below are brief descriptions of the work of several scientists who, through their own tenacity, curiosity, and discipline, developed questions and identified projects that made them famous.

ARCHIMEDES (287–212 B.C.) was a Greek mathematician, physicist, and inventor. He is often called the father of experimental science because he was one of the first scientists to test his ideas by experimentation.

Archimedes was presented with his best-known project by Hiero, king of Syracuse, Sicily, where Archimedes lived. The king had suspicions concerning a new gold crown he had commissioned. He thought the goldsmith had been dishonest and had mixed the gold with a less precious metal. The king called upon Archimedes to discover whether or not the crown was pure.

Archimedes *observed* that all objects of equal weight have the same volume (occupy the same amount of space). He knew, through *classification,* that two pieces of gold, if they were pure and of the same weight, would have the same volume. He knew that one ounce (28 g) of gold would have less volume than one ounce (28 g) of silver, because gold is heavier than silver.

Archimedes then pondered a way to turn his observations into scientific experimentation. The way came to him while he was in the process of taking a bath. The scientist noticed that when he got into a tub full of water, some of the water spilled over the side. He *inferred* that if he captured this overflow in a container and measured it, its volume would equal the weight of his own body.

He set this forth in a *hypothesis* and then moved toward the *testing.* He obtained the crown in question from Hiero and placed it in water. He did the same with an equal weight of pure gold. The gold displaced more water than the crown.

Conclusion: The goldsmith had cheated.

GALILEO GALILEI (1564–1642) was the first of the modern scientists because he broke the hypnotic hold the ancients (Aristotle, etc.) had upon scientific thought. Galileo believed in the use of the senses to formulate new laws and in experimentation to test the accuracy and credibility of his sensory observations. He also believed in the quantification (measuring) of all things, and thus he helped give birth to the scientific method.

Galileo was born in Pisa, Italy. As a young man, he entered the University of Pisa to study philosophy and medicine. A rebel in many ways, Galileo forsook the field of medicine for the study of mathematics and physics. It was in these fields that he disengaged himself from past traditions and moved forward into the unexplored frontiers of scientific discovery.

The young mathematician *observed* that gravity pulls objects, no matter what their weight, to the earth at the same speed. This theory was contrary to Aristotle's theory. He *classified* his observations and then *inferred* that no matter what the height, all objects would fall at the same rate of speed (velocity) discounting air resistance. Thus he formulated the *hypothesis* that all objects, no matter what their density, would fall to the earth at the same speed, and hit the surface at approximately the same time. He *tested* his hypothesis by climbing with two cannon balls to the top of the Leaning Tower of Pisa. One of the balls weighed 10 pounds (4.5 kg), the other weighed 1 pound (.45 kg). Galileo dropped both balls from the top of the tower at the same moment. A crowd of students, professors, and dignitaries observed as the weights struck the earth at approximately the same instant. These results proved Galileo's theory to be correct.

Conclusion: All bodies fall to the earth at the same speed.

LOUIS PASTEUR (1822–1895) was a French chemist born in Dôle, France. He received his degree from the Royal College of Besançon and then entered the Ecole Normale Supérieure school in Paris. In 1847 he received a Ph.D. in science, with a concentration in biology and chemistry.

Dr. Pasteur is famous for many things. The science project described here concerns his discovery of immunization.

After Pasteur discovered that microbes (small bacteria) were the cause of a particular disease in silkworms, French poultry farmers appealed to him to find out why their chickens were being attacked by cholera. Upon isolating the germ that was to blame, the French scientist asked himself, could he find a way to prevent the disease itself, somehow using his knowledge of what was causing the disease?

Pasteur proceeded to do extensive research and to conduct a myriad of experiments on the microbes he had isolated from infected chickens. It was in the fall of 1879 that he accidentally *observed* a phenomenon that led to his discovery of immunization.

Pasteur had been in the country on a vacation. Upon returning to his laboratory, he resumed doing experiments, using cultures of bacteria he had grown the previous spring. He was disturbed to note that chickens previously inoculated failed to get the disease when inoculated with these new cultures.

Based upon his observations, and an *inference* he made, Pasteur developed his *hypothesis* that if an organism is infected by a weakened form of a disease-producing germ, then the individual will develop an immunity to that particular disease.

He tested his hypothesis by weakening various other bacteria in different ways and then using these weakened concoctions to vaccinate organisms against the disease they caused. His first success was with sheep anthrax. He inoculated one group of sheep and left another group alone. The inoculated group lived but the unprotected group succumbed to the disease.

Conclusion: Organisms vaccinated with a weakened strain of certain diseases will, in most cases, develop an immunity to those diseases.

Pasteur's greatest success with immunization came in 1885, when he discovered, after five years of experimentation, a reliable vaccine for the dread disease hydrophobia (rabies).

PIERRE CURIE and **MARIE SKLODOWSKA CURIE** (1859–1906 and 1867–1934) were famous for the discovery of the element radium.

Pierre, a Frenchman and professor at the School of Physics and Chemistry, married the Polish-born Marie when she was a student at the Sorbonne, a university in Paris.

After she married Pierre, Marie began to study the radiation produced by compounds of the element uranium. She insisted that all the uranium compounds she examined were active, yet uranium ore seemed to contain much more radioactivity than could be found in pure uranium. With this *observation,* the Curies set forth on a science project, searching for the source of the excess radiation.

Marie observed that the materials pitchblende and chalcolite gave off more radiation than pure uranium. Thus she *inferred* that these materials must contain an element more radioactive than uranium.

Being poor, the Curies worked in an old leaky shed that served as their laboratory. They suffered many hardships on the path to their great scientific discovery.

After years of experimentation and backbreaking work, the Curies were finally able to isolate from one ton of pitchblende less than 4/1000 of an ounce (an ounce is 28 grams) of a material that glowed and emitted 900 times the radioactivity of pure uranium. They named this new element radium, and in 1903 they received the Nobel Prize in physics for their prodigious science project.

ALBERT EINSTEIN (1879–1955) was born in Ulm, Germany. He studied mathematics and theoretical physics at the Polytechnic Institute in Zurich, Switzerland. After graduation he took a job as a patent examiner in order to support his family, and in his spare time he worked on his mathematical and physical theories.

In 1905 Einstein published a number of papers that seemed to alter the basic concepts of physical science. These included (1) the Quantum Theory; (2) the Inertia of Energy; and (3) the Specific Theory of Relativity. In 1916 Einstein published his General Theory of Relativity, which extended and modified the Specific Theory of Relativity.

In 1921 Einstein received the Nobel Prize in physics for his work, and he was hailed by all as one of the greatest minds the world had ever seen.

The advent of Nazism in the 1930s caused this eminent scientist to flee Germany and come to the United States. The Nazis confiscated all of Einstein's property and revoked his citizenship. In the United States, Einstein accepted a position at the Institute for Advanced Study in Princeton, New Jersey. In 1940 he became a naturalized citizen of the United States.

Over the years, Einstein had *observed* that motion is not absolute but, rather, relative. It changes with the position of the observer. Einstein put forth his premise in a *hypothesis* based on a person riding in a railroad car.

This person on the train opens one of the windows in the car and, while looking out and down, drops a stone from the window. To the person who dropped the stone it looks as if the stone falls straight down (follows a straight path). But to a person standing on the embankment as the train races by, it appears as if the stone follows a curved path earthward.

All things, according to Einstein, are relative. There is within the universe only one thing that is absolute and constant: the velocity (speed) of light as it passes from one segment of the universe to another.

Appendix C.
Sample
Science Projects

1. PROJECTS ON AIR
(FOUR EXPERIMENTS)

Air is matter (has weight, takes up space).

Materials
A yardstick
String
3 balloons
2 soda bottles
Clay
2 funnels
Water
A small jar
A 4" × 4" (10 cm × 10 cm) piece of paper
A small Pyrex flask
Alcohol burner
Ringstand
Pencil
Stick pin

Method
You are now going to do four different experiments. One experiment is to prove air has weight. Another is to prove air takes up space. We said that air exerts pressure. This

pressure is a form of energy. The final two experiments are designed to prove that air pressure is energy.

Experiment I

Take two balloons that are the same size and blow them up to the same size. Tie their necks so that air cannot escape. Tie about a 12″ (30 cm) string to each balloon. *The strings must be the same length.*

Tie a string about 2″ (5 cm) long around the middle of a yardstick or dowel. This string will be used to suspend the yardstick in the air. Tie one balloon to each end of the yardstick. Lift the yardstick in the air and adjust the middle string so that both balloons are balanced. Now take a stick pin and pop one of the balloons. What happened? What does this prove?

Experiment II

Put one of your funnels in the top of a soda bottle. Now take a beaker of water and fill the bottle.

Now take some clay and cover the top of the other soda bottle. Use your pencil to make a hole in the clay. Put the funnel into the bottle through the hole. Push the clay up around the funnel so that air cannot escape from the bottle. Now pour water from the beaker into the funnel. What happens? What does this prove?

Experiment III

Take a small jar and fill it to the very top with water. Now take your 4″ × 4″ (10 cm × 10 cm) piece of paper and cover the top of the jar. Hold the paper over the top of the jar while you turn it upside down. Remove your hand. What happens? What held the paper on the jar? Why?

Experiment IV

Cover the mouth of your small flask with a balloon. Place the flask on a ringstand. Light the alcohol burner under the flask and let it burn for about 2 minutes maximum. Watch carefully for a reaction. What happens? Why?

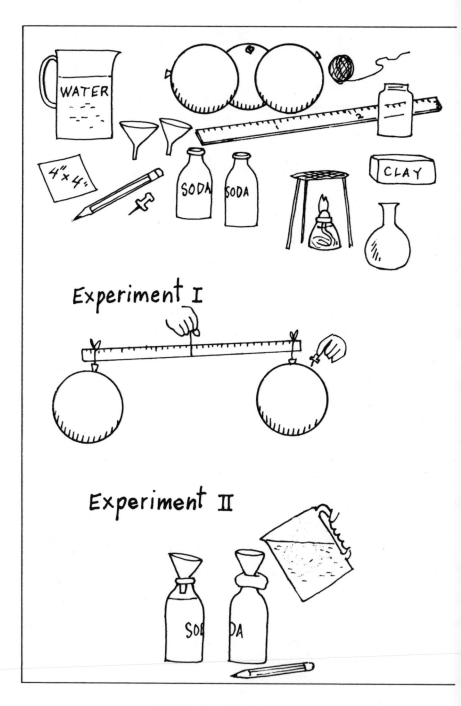

Experiment I

Experiment II

Experiment III

Experiment IV

2. PROJECTS ON PHOTOSYNTHESIS

Plants produce sugar and then change sugar to starch.

As you have learned, plants produce a simple sugar called glucose ($C_6H_{12}O_6$) during the process of photosynthesis. This is the basic food that feeds every living organism on earth. The plant produces sugar and sends it to the rest of the plant via the phloem. The water molecule enters the plant through the roots and root hairs, and it is then transported to the leaf via the xylem.

The light energy harnessed within the plant then splits the water molecule. This is accomplished through the conversion of light energy (in the chloroplasts) into ATP (chemical energy), which is the power source that actually separates the oxygen atom from the hydrogen atoms in the water molecule. Green plants are the only organisms on earth capable of storing and converting light energy to produce food.

Carbon dioxide enters the plant through the stomata of the leaf. This carbon dioxide is very important in the food-making process. Once the water molecule is split, its oxygen atom combines with other oxygen atoms from split water molecules and the pure oxygen exits the leaf through the stomata. This gives us the oxygen we breathe.

The four hydrogen atoms from the two split water molecules work with the carbon dioxide. Two of the hydrogen atoms combine with one oxygen atom to form a water molecule. Water molecules then exit the leaf through the stomata. This process is called *transpiration* (water leaving a plant through the stomata in its leaves).

The remaining hydrogen atoms combine with carbon dioxide molecules to form larger molecules having the same basic properties as the simple substance CH_2O. Eventually, when six carbon dioxide molecules combine with twelve hydrogen atoms, they form a glucose molecule, $C_6H_{12}O_6$, a simple sugar.

The plant takes this sugar and turns it into starch. The plant also makes fat and protein. This is why we can get our necessary protein, starch, fat, and sugar from green plants.

Now we will show some simple tests that prove the occurrence of these processes.

Materials
Test tube
Any green plant
Water
Benedict's solution
Tongs
Alcohol burner
Test-tube rack

Method
Take the stem, leaf, or petiole from a green plant. Put a piece into the test tube and cover it with water. Now add an equal amount of Benedict's solution to the test tube. Boil the solution for about one minute and watch for a reaction. The color the plant turns will tell you how much sugar was in the plant. Put the test tube in the rack when finished.

— a light green indicates
little or no sugar
— yellow indicates
a moderate amount of sugar
— orange or brick-red indicates
a large amount of sugar.

Materials
Several leaves, with petioles,
    from a green plant (geranium)
4 tablespoons sugar
Beaker of water
Petri dish
2 small jars
Scissors

Iodine solution
Pencils
Alcohol lamp
Ringstand
Beaker with alcohol

Method

Cut three geranium leaves from a green plant. Cut the leaves off so that the petioles are intact. Boil *one* of the leaves in alcohol to extract the chlorophyll. Then flood the leaf in the petri dish with iodine solution to test for starch (these leaves should have little or no starch).

Now take the other two leaves with the petioles. Put one leaf in a small jar of water and label it. In the other jar add the water and the sugar. Stir to make a sugar solution. Now put in the remaining leaf. Make sure the petiole dips into the solution. This is how the leaf gets its sugar. Put it in a closet along with the leaf in a jar of water. Each day someone should snip off the tip of the petiole. This will keep the conductive cells open.

Remove both leaves from the jar. Remove chlorophyll from each separate leaf, and then test each one separately with iodine solution for evidence of starch. What are your results?

Index

About the Author

Martin Gutnik is a science teacher and the author of many science books for young readers. His field of specialization is ecology. In this area he has published seven books, numerous articles, and has won several awards for his efforts. This is Mr. Gutnik's second book for Franklin Watts. His first, *The Science of Classification: Finding Order Among Living and Nonliving Objects* (a First Book), was published at the same time as this one. Mr. Gutnik lives in the state of Wisconsin with his family.

507.2
GUT

10849

GUTNIK, MARTIN J.
HOW TO DO A SCIENCE PROJECT AND
REPORT

507.2
GUT

10849

AUTHOR		
GUTNIK, MARTIN J.		
TITLE		
HOW TO DO A SCIENCE PROJECT AND REPORT		
DATE DUE	BORROWER'S NAME	ROOM NUMBER
3-26	Vanessa Wheeler	16
5-25	Dustin	Q
4-27	WARD	C
1-14		

Wh
5-25
D
W
11-1
M
We
4-

10849